To Pastor An.
May God
for your Ministry "Jesus Christ"
will Bring Many Souls To Christ!
I Enjoy and Loot forward →

Behind Enemy Lines
Saved by a Secret Weapon

To Serving God with You and
ushering Souls into The Kingdom
of Heaven.

By Danny Clifford

May God Bless You as You read
This Book — May an anointly
of Compassion for Souls Come over
You
Danny Clifford
2/13/11

XULON
ELITE

You are a
Mighty "Man of God" "Serve Him"

Behind Enemy Lines
Saved by a Secret Weapon
by Danny Clifford

Printed in the United States of America

ISBN 9781612155227

Unless otherwise indicated, Bible quotations are taken from The New International Version of the Bible. Copyright © 2008 by Zondervan publisher.

Edited By: **Nikki Jenkins**
Publishing Consultant: **Donald Newman**

www.xulonpress.com

Dedication

God's Ranger Team of people that He selected to meet and influence my life direction during the past 8 years:

Bishop: Stephen Coleman, my first Pastor, teacher, and mentor.

Prophet: Daniel Senga, my spiritual teacher and mentor, my son.

Michelle: My beautiful wife and best friend.

Jesus: Thank you for enduring the painful price you paid to rescue me. How can I repay you for extracting me up and out of the thick canopy jungle of sin I was in. You are my Secret weapon. You are my Hero, and Medal of Honor Winner.

Acknowledgments

Bishop **Stephen Coleman,** of Williams Temple Church of God in Christ in Portland, Maine, played an important role in my decision to begin a new life with Jesus Christ. If not for Bishop's early Sunday morning Bible studies, where would I be? Bishop Coleman is a strong yet humble teacher of the Word of God, whom I have come to love as my brother, my competitive fishing partner, and my Pastor who conducted our marriage. He loves God and is a compassionate leader for the sheep he leads. I enjoy his teaching and sandwiches while fishing. Thank You for setting the example. In war time, we would call you a pathfinder.

David Thete, I had just dedicated my life to Christ when, one Sunday morning, I was kneeling down at the altar praying and God put this young boy of six years old beside me to pray. As I was praying, I was distracted a bit by his prayer, so I stopped to listen. He was praying a prayer with conviction and faith for other people asking God to help this one and that one. As I listened, I broke down weeping; how could this child care for other people so much, he was praying for others not himself. David, his Mother Adele, and 2 sisters Dorcas, and Marielle, are refugees from the Congo, in Africa. God introduced my wife, Michelle, and I to this family so I could learn what faith really was. Through David, God taught me that I must come to God as a child. David is my son, kind of, and my guardian. When he prays for God to allow us to catch fish, David always gets more fish?

Prophet Daniel Senga is president and founder of Meditation Garden Ministries in Portland, Maine. This heavenly anointed young man is one of the most spiritually gifted men I have ever met in my life. The Holy Spirit has blessed him with Spiritual Gifts some are; Word of Knowledge, Healing, Prophecy, Deliverance, Discernment, and Wisdom beyond that of many old men. God flexes His muscles through this Prophet from the Congo, in Africa, yet he is humble and meek. Prophet Danny is my spiritual mentor, my Tad in the

Spiritual realm. I am blessed, by God, to have a Prophet in my life to guide me, teach me, and help me find my purpose and mission in life.

Heather Clifford; My daughter, who makes me beam with humble pride by the life she lives. I have learned so much from her and never told her how great of a teacher she is. She cares for other people more than she does for herself, always giving of herself until she hurts. She loves God and understands what God put her on earth for.

Pastor Adam Alexander; Tehilla Tabernacle Ministries Westbrook, Maine, a Pastor I respect, a brother, a mentor and friend, whom I have learned from by simply watching and observing while on missions with him in Maine and in Texas with "Hurricane Ike". By knowing and being around Pastor Adam, I now know what it would have been like trying to keep up with the Apostle Paul. Pastor Adam taught me well.

My Wife Michelle; What a blessing that God allowed me to be loved by such a special person to share my life and my love with. I respect Michelle for her love for God and her obedience to God, she is beautiful on the inside, her heart belongs to God, and she is beautiful on the outside. I admire her for being able to love me, for her believing in me, and her gracious attitude, allowing me the time to dedicate to this book. Without her encouragement, her smiles, her prayers, and her understanding, this book would not have been written. I love you more than you'll ever know. Thank you for being my friend and my wife.

To Jesus; Our secret weapon, the Savior of the World, author of the Word, and God in the flesh; and The Holy Spirit of "the Great I AM" who taught me and guided me on how to put the material together exactly where He wanted it placed and how He wanted it spoken.

Reviews

*P*rofound: *It's a very interesting read;* Love how you added both worlds of Vietnam combat and the real world where we're at war with the enemy and need to heavily depend on the Spirit of God to stand in this angry world. Hence, even when the storms rage, we have nothing to be afraid of if we walk in His steps and talk His talk.

I loved reading this and seeing how well you connected your point's brother Danny. I have been encouraged and reminded about the awesomeness and how powerful my Jesus is. *This book is a tool that is needed* to point some to Jesus; it also encourages the believer that we win in Jesus and that He is the commander in chief of our lives.

The memories you left embedded in my mind are; to follow your commander in chief's every move E.g.

Imitate how he eats, walk like he walks, talk like he talks, and to let him lead in combat; it drives home the importance of relying heavily on your leader for survival in an uncertain world!

Thank you for taking time to write this. It's packed with God's truths. God bless you as you endeavor to publish this and share it with the world. Keep up the good work and let the world hear and know that Jesus saves through this material. *Bravo!* God Bless.

Annie Mvula

"Behind Enemy Lines Saved by a Secret Weapon" *is fantastic.* I have never been in a battle that contained guns and the possibility of losing my life, but life situations have sometimes felt like a battle. Knowing that there is a plan and purpose and seeing it working in your life is a great inspiration for me. Thank you for sharing and for allowing God to pour into you the words that have flowed so elegantly in your writing that reveals His love for all mankind.

Deborah Dennison Limerick, Maine

My Nephew; Griffin says: *Amazing, shocking, incredible, and moving.* This book kept my interest all the way through with its constant flow, it is an intriguing story, and the remarkable way the author tied actual war into spiritual war is awesome. It is a must read for anyone who wants to know more about God, or just a friend who needs to know Christ. *This book overall is a **five star** to me.* It was well written with an incredible flow and a great tie between the topics of war training and God's army! **A MUST READ!!**

Griffin Clifford, 13 years old

What an uplifting testimony to one's reality of life. If one has never experienced actual warfare, perhaps it would be hard to digest the meaning of all that the author wants so desperately to convey. He has literally found a way to express the many plights that engulfed him while serving his country in the perils of the Vietnam War with the same plights that so easily beset so many people today. The only difference is that the warfare he faces today is fought in the spirit world.

Beverly Cooper-Pete

I found this book breathtaking and very powerful. I enjoyed having the verse location published with the verses, they were right on target and I could revert back to the scriptures and learn more. Thank you for writing this book, it helped me understand so much more about life.

Cindy

Contents

Author Introduction

To survive in Vietnam and come home alive, it required elite training, strong belief in our training, mental and physical repetition of the training, and real true relationships. If we got distracted, failed to pay attention, disobeyed, ignored, or forgot what we were there to do, our percentage of surviving was greatly reduce.

Believe me, there were many things to distract us. Our minds and bodies got hooked up or addicted to drugs, alcohol, sex, the thrill of living on the edge, these are but a few of what was available to destroy us, before we even went on a mission to face what our enemies had for us or the snakes, diseases, and animals of the jungle.

This book tells a very interesting, exciting, and intriguing story of my training, experiences, relationships, and firsthand knowledge as a United States Army Staff Sergeant with the 75th Airborne Rangers in 1969 and 1970, performing reconnaissance missions behind enemy lines. And in 1971, serving as a ranger advisor with the 2nd Ranger Command in the mountainous jungle region of border camp number six at village Plei Mrong, South Vietnam near the Cambodian border. My mission was teaching and training Mountain Yard and Vietnamese soldiers in ranger warfare techniques and assisting them in relocating civilian villagers that were being plundered by the enemy.

When I arrived, in November, at Company 75th Airborne Ranger, the first thing I needed to do was to de-program myself of most of the training I had received from the Army prior to arriving in Vietnam. For example; I had been taught to always ambush from the high ground; that high ground determined the actual site selection for an ambush.

De-program that training; it sounded good and worked in World War II and Korea, but this was guerilla warfare. Tad taught us first to monitor a trail by observing how the enemy was traveling on the trail.

Once the direction of travel was known, always set the ambush on the right hand side of the trail according to the enemy's route of March, regardless of the height of the terrain.

The reason is that most people, about 90 %, are right handed and the enemy's weapons would be pointed away from you as you set off the ambush. After a few hours, any soldier running missions in the hot jungles of Southeast Asia would have their attention span, focus, alertness, and weapons positions drop off measurably, especially while they traveled through what they perceived as their own safe territory. This means that when you ambush to the right of the trail, five Rangers would fire a full 20 round magazine from an M-16 rifle in 2.3 seconds.

That's 100 bullets into a kill zone while the enemy freezes up for a second in shock from all the firing. Once they realize what is happening, they fall to the ground turning their weapons from the left to the right and try to locate where the firing is coming from. That just took 2.8 seconds and our hands are on the detonators of five claymore mines. Each mine has hundreds of shrapnel like bee bees packed into them and about a pound of C-4 explosive. The enemy's rifle hasn't gotten to their shoulder yet to fire. We detonate the claymore mines, if needed, and the enemy; well that's why it's called an ambush. The sixth person, a Ranger radio operator, was behind us guarding our back with the radio and already our choppers and support were coming.

This story takes you from physical warfare to Spiritual warfare in such a way that your faith will be renewed and will help you with questions about the spirit realm and the spiritual warfare that goes on daily for our souls. My prayer is that it sheds light on the battle between good (God) and evil (Satan).

Sit back and enjoy this short, powerful story. My mission is that when you reach the end of this book, you will have been introduced face to face with Jesus. Enhancing your understanding of why Jesus did what He did. He loves you and wants to have a relationship with you. One that will change you, from who you are now, to a brand new person. You are the Soul, purpose of this book.

Author Danny Clifford

Foreword

First, I would like to thank God Almighty for the work, desire, passion and anointing He has placed upon and within you. I've had the privilege of not only watching the Holy Spirit water the many seeds that have been planted inside your heart throughout your lifetime, but also experiencing firsthand the unveiling of spiritual revelations regarding the Word as you've gone from a baby drinking milk to a man digesting food of substance.

This is the beginning of many things God has appointed for your journey called life, as you start a process of sharing and releasing the Gospel to those who may not have heard or known the Truth.

Thank you for being my friend, my husband, my teacher and my covering.

With Love,

-Michelle

1 Timothy 2:3-7 (New King James Version)

For this is good and acceptable in the sight of God our Savior, who desires all men to be saved and to come to the knowledge of the truth. For there is one God and one Mediator between God and men, the Man Christ Jesus, who gave Himself a ransom for all, to be testified in due time, for which I was appointed a preacher and an apostle - I am speaking the truth in Christ and not lying - a teacher of the Gentiles in faith and truth.

Behind Enemy Lines
Saved by a Secret Weapon

From Oct 1969 to May 1971, I was in the U. S. Army fighting a war in Vietnam.

In war, no matter what your job is, all you witness is death and destruction. You take territory, kill or get killed, capture prisoners, or become one. Survival depends on the relationships you establish, the reality of the training you receive, your confidence in your training and the effective use of your training. Warfare is not a game; without utilizing your training, in war you will die. If you allow your head, body, and heart, to be influenced by anything other than your readiness for action, your chances of survival are greatly reduced.

When I arrived in Vietnam, I had orders to go to the 173rd Airborne Brigade. While I was waiting for travel orders, a team of Army Rangers visited the soldiers who had just arrived in Vietnam from the United States. They were there to recruit volunteers for the 75th Airborne Ranger Battalion. The Ranger Battalion had a company of about 150 men attached to each army division throughout Vietnam, tasked with providing up to date enemy information. I went along to listen to what they had to say.

They explained that the purpose of Ranger Teams in Vietnam was to conduct reconnaissance missions. A Ranger team consisted of six men sent out deep into enemy territory, in their back yard, usually for four days and three nights, very quietly exploring an area of about 4 to 6 square miles.

Each mission had three possible outcomes, different ways. Ideally, it would be concluded peacefully and the Rangers would be extracted peacefully at the end of four days. We could set up an ambush in an attempt to capture a P. O. W. which would compromise our location, and we would need to be extracted immediately. Finally, the most dangerous way to end a mission would result from a Ranger team being ambushed. In such a scenario, we would run like crazy until we could communicate our situation by radio and request support from F-4 Jet Air-strikes and/or helicopter gunships so that we could be extracted to relative safety.

The most feared end to a mission for a Ranger team was being ambushed at night while sleeping. To avoid such a nasty surprise, we always set up trip flares to warn us of an enemy pursuing us and claymore mines aimed at covering the area where the flares were set. When a flare went up, we would detonate the claymore mines and, as quiet as possible, run using a pre-planned escape route. The rule of engagement at night was not to use our rifles, as the muzzle flash would give our location away. While running, the first call we made was to our secret night time weapon.

"Puff the Magic Dragon" was available to us; a C-130 large cargo airplane with an ordinance of several mini-guns aboard and each mini gun was capable of firing 5,000 rounds per minute. That's putting a bullet in every square inch of a football field in a matter of seconds. One of the most intimidating weapons I have ever seen because every fourth round was a tracer. At night, it looked like a stream of fire coming from heaven to earth, with a continuous sound of a burrrrrrrp; that's why it got the name "Puff the Magic Dragon". The worst nightmare the enemy could have.

Once a Ranger team's mission is compromised, they need to be extracted. They may need any combination of support and fire power, we just discussed, to get extracted. Extract means a single helicopter making a fast approach to an open landing zone swooping to the ground. The only protection the chopper had for those long seconds of open exposure while approaching, hovering and taking back off from an open landing zone, was two M-60 machine guns, one on each side of the chopper. The chopper would swoop in (hovering up and down from 2 to 5 feet from the ground for just a brief moment) while six Rangers would run and jump in through the open doors of the chopper, then it would lift off as fast as possible to avoid being hit by enemy gunfire.

In dense jungle canopy where no open LZ was available, the helicopter would attach a rope ladder that would be dropped down through an opening in the canopy. The team waiting on the ground would take their half inch nylon rope with their steel snap link attached to their rucksack and tie a repelling seat around their waist behind their backside, up through their groin then tie off a square knot by their belly and take a single 3/8 inch D shaped steel snap link and snap it into the knot. Then the Rangers would climb up the swinging rope ladder attached to the hovering chopper, snap the steel D link over the metal rung of the rope ladder and be heisted up out of harm's way swinging back and forth in the air while being transported back to home base 1500 to 2000 feet above the ground.

At the close of the Ranger's presentation, they told us we would be trained by the very best reconnaissance personnel the Army had. Once trained, if we took the training to heart, performing the training would be an everyday occurrence for us. If we didn't take the training to heart, well, they didn't finish the sentence.

They bragged how good the food was, dehydrated light weight LRRP rations (Long Range Recognizance Patrol), just add water and you had your choice of the best chili and beans or chicken and rice.

The final closing presentation was rewards and bonuses. After each mission, we would have 3 days to stand down and recover to prepare for the next mission. The Rangers also had a bonus and rewards program that gave us additional time off for capturing P O W's (prisoners of war) alive or capturing important documents. I volunteered. I've always been a sucker for volunteering.

When I arrived at November Company 75th Airborne Rangers, I'll never forget the training I received from a Hawaiian Staff Sergeant, we'll call him Tad. The training was real. The first thing I needed to do was de-program myself from most of the training I had received from the Army.

For example, in my previous training I had been taught to always ambush from high ground and that high ground determined the actual site selection for an ambush. I needed to De-program that training; it sounded good and it worked in World War II. But Tad taught us first, to monitor a trail by observing how the enemy was traveling on the trail. Once the direction of travel was known, always set the ambush on the right hand side of the trail according to the enemy's route of march, regardless of the height of the terrain.

The reason being is that most people, about 90 %, are right handed and the enemies' weapons would be pointed away from you as you set off the ambush.

Any soldier running missions in the hot jungles of Southeast Asia, after a few hours, their attention span, focus, alertness, and weapons positions drop off measurably, especially while they travel through what they perceive as their own safe territory. This means that when you ambush to the right of the trail, five Rangers would fire a full 20 round magazine from an M-16 rifle in 2.3 seconds. That's 100 bullets into a kill zone while the enemy freezes up for a second, in shock, from all the firing. Once they realize what is happening, they fall to the ground turning their weapons from the left to the right trying to locate where the firing is coming from. That just took 2.8 seconds and our hands are on the detonators of five claymore mines. Each mine has hundreds of buck shots packed into them with about a pound of C-4 explosives and the enemies' rifle hasn't gotten to their shoulder yet to fire. We detonate the claymore mines, if needed, and the enemy; well that's why it's called an ambush. The sixth person, the Ranger Radio Operator, was behind us guarding our back with the radio and already our choppers and support are coming.

It was Tad's training, his leadership and God's grace, which helped me survive through the missions, booby traps, and escape ambushes. It was up to me to choose to believe and put into action Tad's teachings. I could have rejected them and sat through them and done nothing. By preparing and doing what I was taught, it prepared me for what was to come.

Tad had been in Vietnam for almost 4 years when I arrived. He had more personal confirmed kills of the enemy than any American soldier in all the Armed Services. He spoke fluent Mountain Yard and fluent Vietnamese. He had never had a person wounded or killed on his team, but he had been wounded three times receiving three Purple Hearts. He walked point; he lead and his team followed him.

Tad would eat like the enemy, he carried an AK-47 rifle like they used. He dressed just like the enemy dressed, either Viet Cong black P J's with a straw hat, or a North Vietnamese Regular Army uniform, and he always walked point; out in front of the team, the lead person and they followed him.

Our enemies were experts in setting booby traps and camouflaging them so you couldn't see them. They used natural things from the jungle such as vines and trees; alive and dead, to hide the grenades, claymore mines, and other explosive devices. They would put the booby traps where you would least expect them and were almost impossible to see. During Tad's training, he repeated many times, "Follow me, walk where I walk, imitate my movements, and you'll be safe."

Tad looked exactly like an enemy, and on one occasion, an enemy soldier spoke to him while walking point, telling Tad to get out of the way quickly because there was an American patrol right behind him that they were going to ambush. Tad trained me in Vietnam and yes, the training was good and it was real. Not ritualistic. I had a mentor that I believed in. I obeyed his teachings and trainings. Why? Because in four years nobody had been killed or even wounded while running missions with him. Around 200 missions behind enemy lines and nobody killed or wounded. I believed if I did what he did, I would be coming home alive and whole.

Before we ever went on a mission, we gathered all the information we could regarding how many enemy forces were in the territory we were going into. How they traveled and operated, their type of weapons, and what was their purpose for being at that location. We needed to know everything we could about our enemy before we went on a mission. Without this knowledge our chances of survival were greatly diminished, because we were operating on their home turf.

There have been occasions, while on missions, when I thought things were hopeless for our survival, but just when I thought we were finished, help arrived.

By God's grace, I survived one and one-half years in Vietnam. All the drugs, alcohol, fire-fights, snakes, grenades, booby traps, missions, all that the enemy had in schemes and ambushes to kill me, God sustained me; because of my mother, sister and brother's prayers.

I say by God's grace because I was 19-21 years old at the time I was in Vietnam. I had been brought up by a mother who feared, loved and obeyed God. She brought me up, from a baby, in a Bible believing church. When I was 13, I was looking at Bible colleges to attend after high school, to become the next Billy Graham or Reinhard Bonnke.

It was late in my freshman year of high school when I decided to trade in my loyalty to God for high school popularity, girls, sports stardom, and being accepted by my new friends and the world. I ran away from God, I turned my back on Him and I cheated on Him. My relationship with God changed. God wanted to have a relationship with me; I just wanted to have an affair with God whenever I needed Him.

I acted like I was happy with my new life. I became real good at making believe and fooling others. I even told them how great it was, but it wasn't. I knew what perception was and I knew what the truth was. That's why I say by the grace of God I am alive, whole, and with a sound mind. I don't ever remember getting on my knees thanking Him for all that He did for me during those 18 months.

In summary, it took real true training from someone who had experienced and survived what he taught. It took building relationships with helicopter pilots, who risked their life to come and get us during rain storms in a mountainous area with extremely low clouds, while we ran from the enemy who outnumbered us. We knew it was impossible for a chopper to break through the low ceiling of clouds in the mountainous area, but they did it. Beer, sodas, and steaks were a great relationship builder and a good way to say thank you.

The people I allowed to influence me, those that I hung out with, everything that I allowed to come in contact with me had an effect on my survival. If I allowed drugs or alcohol to take up my time instead of resting and learning about my next mission, who the enemy is and how they moved and operated, I knew that it would have a negative impact on what would happen on the next assignment. I needed to be prepared at all times. ***Physical warfare is real.*** Our enemy we faced was real. The bullets were real. There were thousands of them and they believed in what they were taught. They acted on their belief and soldiers and civilians were killed and wounded, land was conquered and a new nation was born. This really happened. We can see, we can hear, and we can feel the effects of physical war so we know it's real. I came back home from Vietnam alive, hardly a scratch on my body. While over 58,267 American soldiers were killed in action, 303,644 American soldiers were wounded in action in Vietnam and over 1500 soldiers missing in action. My believing and being obedient to what I was taught made a difference in me living or dying.

Know Your Enemy

Is *the Spiritual Realm Real?* The spiritual realm is a real unseen existence, alive and active. We humans cannot hear and we cannot see in the spiritual realm. So, because we can't see, hear, or touch, we don't think about it and some people don't even believe in a spiritual realm. They believe it's a figment of someone's imagination.

Spiritual life is not understood by even the wisest of humans because we have a flesh body. The senses of our flesh do not have the ability to operate in the spiritual world, unless God permits us spiritually to do so, or unless you are controlled by the devil.

Is Spiritual Warfare Real? There really is a war going on right now with Satan and his demonic spirits (evil) against God, His angels and praying saints (Good). Every day, we are constantly being influenced, set-up, ambushed, attacked, and tempted by evil spirits. Satan is in control of the world. He is the prince of this world today and will be until Jesus Christ returns at the end of the tribulation period.

We know that we are children of God, and that the whole world is under the control of the evil one. I John 5:19.

We must understand and recognize that the very air about us is filled with hostile forces that have succeeded in keeping you from having a relationship with God.

For those who are God's children, Satan is constantly attempting to destroy our fellowship with God and to deprive us, to cut us off from our source and starve us, to severe us from the vine that nourishes us.

This war is for the possession of your soul. The battle ground is your mind, your will, your emotions and to dominate your unredeemed soul. Paul tells us, "*For our struggle is not against flesh and blood, but against the rulers, against the authorities, against the powers of this dark world and against the spiritual forces of evil in the heavenly realms.*" Ephesians 6:12.

Satan and his demonic angels, powers, and sin, is much more powerful than humans. We need to know as much about our enemy as possible in order to survive. God's Word teaches us everything we need to know.

Persons who don't really know what they believe, persons who don't believe and persons who selectively believe some, but not all, of the Gospel of Jesus Christ; these people are all under the control of Satan, who is the prince of this world. Almost all of them are unaware of whose spiritual contract they fall under. Some of them are in pulpits preaching. Satan truly is more powerful than human non-believers.

Lucifer, whose aliases are Satan, the serpent, the wicked one, and the devil, is a created being, a fallen cherub (angel), who became twisted on the inside. Satan was a very powerful arch angel serving God before he was cast out of heaven.

The power the devil has is the power you give him by believing his lies. These lies are like a trap, or a snare, that take people captive. Most people don't even realize when they are deceived or ensnared, that is how slick and devious the devil is.

Paul tells us, "*And no wonder, for Satan himself masquerades as an angel of light. It is not surprising, then, if his servants masquerade as servants of righteousness. Their end will be what their actions deserve.*" II Corinthians 11:14-15.

Jesus told us, "*... He was a murderer from the beginning, not holding to the truth, for there is no truth in him. When he lies, he speaks his native language, for he is a liar and the father of lies.*" John 8:44.

The devil and his evil followers on this planet are always trying to draw you and me away from our Heavenly Father, trying to destroy our relationship with Him and God's plan for our lives.

Pride is one of Satan's Most Powerful and Most Popular weapons. And we love this bait. Pride is a powerfully deceptive spirit for Satan to use against us because it blinds us from God. It blinds us from the reality that we even need God. The most dangerous sin in people, that allows blindness to occur, is pride.

Most of us live by the flesh, pride of the flesh; it is not of the Spirit of God. Pride tells us that we can do things without God's help or intervention. That is why it is so dangerous. Through pride, we become blinded, set in our minds and hearts, we become hard-hearted and rebellious against or opposing God. Pride blinds us to God.

When blinded like that, we can believe a lie or think we are okay even when we are not. **God is the turning point**, the turning around place, is <u>in Him</u>! We need God's help! We need God!

The sole purpose of Satan and his forces is to maim us, to inflect wounds on us, to discourage us, so we will lose heart and fall out of fellowship with the Father. Once the relationship breaks down just a little bit, we slack off on our praying, our reading, and mediation then revelations, visions, and dreams are not with us and then our relationship with God is strained. We start throwing the blame on God just like we do in our marriage, relationships or with others we love, we start blaming them.

Then Satan, like a lion, stalks us and when he finds us weak enough, he tries to separate us even more. We become like a single prey, separated from the rest of the group. We stopped our relationship with God and are fully exposed to the lion. We are very vulnerable at this point spiritually. This is a "Kill Zone." The disciple Peter told us to, "*Be self-controlled and alert. Your enemy the devil prowls around like a roaring lion looking for someone to devour. Resist him, standing firm in the faith, because you know that your brothers throughout the world are undergoing the same kind of sufferings.*" I Peter 5:8-9.

Ambushed and Taken Prisoner of War

How did this Spiritual War begin? *How did Satan become in charge of us?* I thought that God created the world and God was in control of everything. How did this all start? This war started in the beginning. Originally, God created us exactly like Himself. God is Spirit, Holy, and without sin. God said, *"Let us make man in our image, in our likeness. So God created man in his own image, in the image of God he created him; male and female he created them."* Genesis 1:26-27.

We are a ***spirit being*** created in the image and likeness of God with an outer shell of flesh that contains our spirit. The purpose of man's spirit is to communicate with God's Spirit and in turn communicate what the Holy Spirit says to ***our soul*** … and body.

Our body or flesh includes my mind. We are very sensitive to the physical surroundings of the world and the senses of natural the things of our body; for example - sight, hearing, smell, touch, and taste. Everything we process goes through our mind. Our body seeks to be pleased.

The body communicates to ***the soul*** the natural things of the world and thoughts, our hidden desires of the body and all the physical things. That's why the Bible calls it "things of the flesh".

Our soul, also known as the heart of man, is confined in the body. The soul of man is the real me and you - our personalities, likes, dislikes, and attitudes.

The Soul of Man is the referee or the decision making part of us humans. The soul decides either to go with what man's spirit communicates to the soul, which is from God, or the soul could decide to go with what the body communicates to it, which comes from the natural flesh of man. This process of decision making we refer to as our free will.

Our Free Will is an independent free will. Free to choose, to say, and to do, what we desire to do. Even when we chose to disobey God, He honors our will because He must honor our will.

Initially, God's intentions were clear. He gave Adam and Eve and their descendant's dominion and authority over the entire earth and all creation. God put Adam here to be His representative.

God confirms this in Psalms 115:16, *"The highest heavens belong to the LORD, but the earth he has given to man."* God didn't give ownership of the earth to humanity, but He assigned the responsibility of governing it to humanity. Adam was God's governor on Earth.

God put His very life and Spirit into us. He communed with us; we were His children and He was our Father. Adam had a direct relationship with God and Adam enjoyed being in the Garden of Eden in God's presence. God commanded Adam, *"You are free to eat from any tree in the garden; but you must not eat from the tree of the knowledge of good and evil, for when you eat of it you will surely die."* Genesis 2: 16-17.

God wanted a family of sons and daughters who could personally relate to Him and Him to them. So He made our original parents similar to Himself. So much so, that God enabled man and woman to re-produce spiritual beings *"Has not the LORD made them one? In flesh and spirit they are his. And why one? Because he was seeking godly offspring."* Malachi 2:15.

Sin – Enters Humanity. The serpent was craftier than any of the animals the Lord had made and deceived Eve into eating from the forbidden tree. When Eve gave it to Adam and Adam ate the forbidden fruit, a sinful nature entered into Adam and Eve physically and spiritually. Because of their rebellion against God, sin entered our ancestors spiritually and ended up manifesting itself in our physical bodies.

God had no choice but to remove Adam and Eve from the garden. Our relationship with God was severed. God is Holy and cannot co-exist with sin.

We have no idea the predicament we put God in! Once Adam and Eve sinned, their souls were separated from God because of sin. God loved us so much that He removed us from the garden before we had a chance to eat fruit from the Tree of Life.

If Adam and Eve would have eaten from the Tree of Life after they had sinned, that would mean they would live forever in the state of sin that they were in. There would be no way for God to redeem us. No way for the remission of sin. So, God drove Adam and Eve quickly from the garden.

Why is God so opposed to Sin? God is Holy and there is no way for God and sin to co-exist. Holy is a characteristic unique to God's nature. God's name is Holy. Holiness is the fullness and completeness of God. God, as Holy, is separated from humans, God, as a person, is related in **love** to people. Holiness is something that is set apart for God. Holy defines the goodness of God. Yet, God's love desires our redemption.

Sin Keeps Us Separated from God. When Adam and Eve sinned, humanity lost our relationship with God; the ability to walk and talk with God was gone. The peace and joy was gone. The loving closeness was gone. The relationship with God was gone.

Why? The very purpose of our meaningfulness to God was shattered. God created us for the purpose of having a righteous relationship with Him, without sin. Now a discrepancy exists between who we are and who God created us to be. **God and sin never have and never will coexist**.

Not only are we separated from God, Adam also ended up losing his representation status. Let me explain. So complete and final was Adam's authority over the earth that Adam had the ability to give it away to another. Adam made a choice that affected all humanity. The authority that God entrusted to Adam, Adam ended up giving it away to Satan.

In Luke 4:5-6, Jesus is in the desert wilderness fasting and Satan approaches Him and takes Jesus high up and shows Him all the kingdoms of the world in an instant. Satan then says to Jesus *"I will give you all their authority and splendor; for it is mine to give to whomever I want to, If you but bow down and worship me."* Jesus didn't argue with Satan. Jesus knew that Satan, for once, was speaking the truth. Satan had deceived Eve and Adam in the Garden of Eden for it.

Sin – Brought Death

Until God spoke in Genesis 3:19, there was no physical death for humans. So sin brought God's covenant of death to us physically. From the moment of sin in Genesis until today, we have all sinned. *"For all have sinned and fallen short of the glory of God."* Romans

3:23. *"For the wages of sin is death..."* Romans 6:23. This is a physical death, but more importantly, a spiritual death.

Today, many people believe the most important thing, to them, is living and once death occurs, that life stops existing. We really don't think about death and life after death in the spiritual realm. We are not prepared for it and many of us don't even care. The world we live in has convinced us that we are just fleshy human bodies and all there really is to life is what's on this earth, so enjoying it to the fullest is their motto.

Our belief and actions, while on planet earth, will determine our destination for either an eternal life with God or a life of destruction in hell. Someone not believing it simply means they are lost.

Where does this leave us today? People today are not concerned about their separation from God. We shouldn't be shocked when we see and hear our family and friends tell us they don't care about life after death. They have no thoughts and beliefs about eternal life after we die.

Some even ask, "How can we be declared guilty for something Adam did thousands of years ago?" Many feel it isn't fair for God to judge us because of Adam's sin. Yet, each of us confirms our heritage with Adam by our own sins every day. We have the same sinful nature and are prone to rebel against God. We are judged for the sins we commit because we are sinners. We are born from our mother's womb with a sinful nature.

It isn't fairness we need, it is mercy. All of us have reaped the results of Adam's sin. We have inherited his guilt, a sinful nature, the tendency to sin, and God's punishment for sin *"for all have sinned and fall short of the glory of God."* Romans 3:23.

God's covenant with Adam is broken; sin is now over the earth and sin has manifested itself in the human body. God and sin cannot co-exist. Our relationship with God is destroyed because of our rebellious nature toward God.

Today the powers of sin are stronger than we are. We have become enslaved in a sinful nature. Jesus said, *"I tell you the truth everyone who sins is a slave to sin."* John 8:34. The Bible tells us,"*... that the whole world is a prisoner to sin..."* Galatians 3:22.

Paul, speaking of the spiritual power of sin, says it this way, *"I know that nothing good lives in me, that is, in my sinful nature. For I have the desire to do what is good, but I cannot carry it out."* Romans 7:18.

"For the sinful nature desires what is contrary to the Spirit and the Spirit what is contrary to the sinful nature. They are in conflict with each other, so that you do not do what you want." Galatians 5:17.

One Way to be Saved and Rescued

*T**he only hope we have** is if we could start over a-new. If we could somehow re-establish our relationship with God, then that would mean somehow our sin and our rebellious sinful nature would need to be removed from us because God and sin cannot co-exist.

Wouldn't it be nice if we could start all over again? This is the purpose of Jesus coming to planet earth. Jesus is all about God's **Love** and **His Provision** of **forgiveness for us.**

The only source of power over Satan and his demonic host is - in the name of Jesus. The most powerful secret weapon known to humans today is Jesus. He is our C-130, "Puff the Magic Dragon" and He is our extraction chopper.

At Calvary 2000 years ago, Jesus was crucified on the cross, all the horrific sin of the entire world was heaved on Him, and He was carrying the sickness and diseases of the entire world.

Jesus took our place, our death sentence for sin, so we could be forgiven and set free from the bondage of sin and Satan's works. As Jesus was hanging, dying on the cross, just as Jesus began to say, "It is finished", and just before His last breath as He gave up His Spirit, Satan was dancing, thinking he had won and had killed Jesus, "The Son Of God".

Satan thought he was more superior on the earth than Jesus was because Satan had the authority and dominion of the world. He had received it when he deceived Adam in the Garden of Eden. That's when Satan became the Prince of this World. Satan had tried several times to kill Jesus, but never could quite make it happen; somehow Jesus always escaped. Now it's finally happened, Satan is extremely happy, he has achieved his goal; he has Jesus right where he wants him - nailed to a Cross on the edge of death, one breath away.

Satan didn't have a clue that God had orchestrated this spectacular plan of sending His only son Jesus to die as a perfect sacrifice, one time, to pay the ransom for all human sin. This sacrifice was pleasing to God; so much so that God accepted it as the once and for all atonement for all humanities sin against God; total forgiveness.

The day Jesus was crucified was the first day of Passover; this was a very special week of festivities for the Jews. The Jewish law required all activity to cease by the end of the day (about 6:00PM).

The Passover, remember, is in celebration of God delivering the children of Israel and Moses out from the bondage of Egyptian slavery. About 1500 years after Moses lead the children of Israel out of Egypt, on exactly the same day, Jesus Christ is being crucified as a death penalty to set you and I free from the burden and bondage of our slavery to sin and Satan. What timing God has!

It's about 9:00 in the morning as Jesus is being nailed to a cross. Jesus had received no rest the night before because He had been beaten with fist, staffs, punched, kicked, whipped with a barbed tipped whip, and crowned with thorns, all during the night before. As a result of being beaten all night, Jesus died sooner than the two criminals that were crucified with Him. Jesus died about 3:00 P.M.

Shortly after Jesus died, the Roman soldiers broke the legs of the two criminals that were crucified with Him to ensure they would die quickly. The reason for breaking the legs was to stop them from using their legs to push themselves up and breath. Once the legs were broken, the pain was too severe to push them up so they would suffocate and die sooner.

When they came to Jesus, He appeared to be dead. Instead of breaking His legs, one of the Roman soldiers, who were marksmen with spears and swords, took his spear and drove it up into Jesus' body piercing the heart. Blood and water flowed out of His heart; the soldier did this to ensure Jesus was dead. Because it was the Passover, they needed to complete these crucifixions and have the bodies off the crosses and into their graves before the end of the day.

All of a sudden, Satan began to realize what was happening. Satan had no idea until Jesus breathed out His final breath saying, "it is finished", as soon as he gave up His Spirit, things began to happen. Satan thought his plan to kill Jesus was successful, but he soon realized that he was in an ambush. An ambush that would destroy him, that would condemn him and one that would paralyze him.

God's new will took place right before Satan's eyes and there was nothing he could do about it. Satan suddenly realized he had made the mistake of his existence, the biggest of his reign on planet earth, one he would never recover from. The spiritual battle became so violent that it manifested into the physical, the earth shook violently, so much so that the tombs broke open and bodies of many holy saints came to life. The rocks split and when the Roman soldiers saw this, they were terrified and cried out. *"Surely He was the Son of God!"* (Read Matthew 27:50-54).

When Jesus' body was removed from that wooden cross, all of His blood had been shed from the many wounds covering His entire body. They laid the body of Jesus to rest in a tomb.

Spiritually, Jesus carried all the sins of the world into the grave, into the dark regions along with the infirmities and sickness of the world.

Jesus stands as the Master and the Ruler of the Universe. On the 3rd day, when God's cry reached the dark regions, Jesus arose, hurled back the host of darkness and met Satan in an awful battle. Satan was knocked out cold. There was no decision. Jesus just destroyed Satan's works, his principalities, his powers and his strongholds over humanity.

In Hebrews it says, *"Since the children have flesh and blood, he too shared in their humanity so that by his death he might destroy him who holds the power of death—that is, the devil"* (Hebrews 2:14).

That through death, He might destroy and paralyze him that held the dominion of death that is the devil. In other words, after Jesus had put off from Himself the demonic forces and the awful burden of sin, diseases and sickness that He carried with Him down there, He grappled with Satan, conquered him and left him paralyzed, whipped, and defeated. In Luke we read, *"When a strong man, fully armed, guards his own house, his possessions are safe. But when someone stronger attacks and overpowers him, he takes away the armor in which the man trusted and divides up the spoils."* (Luke 11: 21-22)

When Christ arose from the dead, He not only had the keys of death and hell, but He had the very armor in which Satan trusted.

Jesus has defeated the devil. He has defeated all hell, and He stands before the three worlds – Heaven, Earth and Hell as the undisputed victor over Man's ancient destroyer - Satan and sin.

Is it any wonder, that fresh from such a tremendous victory, He should say to His disciples, *"All authority in heaven and on earth has been given to me."* Matthew 28:18; and in Revelations, when John was taken up by the spirit, Jesus said, *"I am the Living One; I was dead, and behold I am alive forever and ever! And I hold the keys of death and Hade*s." (Revelations 1:18).

Extraction by Un-conditional Surrender

I f we surrender our life totally to Jesus, trust Him, His teachings, living and obeying them, we will *have no fear of death. When we turn from our sinful ways here on Earth and accept God's free gift,* our first death is death to sin, while we are alive on earth. We die to the sinful nature and take on the Holy Spirit of God in us. If we die to sin, then we have no fear of a second death because we belong to Christ. A second death for us is our Homecoming into paradise.

One of the two criminals crucified with Jesus said, *"Jesus, remember me when you come into your kingdom."* Jesus told him, *"… today you will be with me in paradise."* Luke 23:42-43.

Our relationship with God the Father is through Jesus Christ and it is conditional; based on 2 critical teachings of Jesus while He was here on earth:

1.) *Our Belief*: What we believe while alive here on earth will determine our destination in eternity; *Jesus said believe in me and my teachings.*

2.) *Our Actions*: While on earth will determine our rewards in heaven or our restitution in hell; *Jesus said follow me: walk as I walk: Imitate me.*

This is why the shedding of the Pure Blood of Jesus Christ on the Cross is vital! Nothing on earth is as important! If we believe that Jesus Christ is the Son of God who died on the cross, was buried, and God raised Him from the dead; if we ask Jesus to come into our heart to cleanse us from the sins we have committed against God, then we are saved. Born a-new, born again and we will be raised up with Christ to be with Him forever. Paul tells us, "*Once you were alienated from God and were enemies in your minds because of your evil behavior. But now he has reconciled you by Christ's physical body through death to present you holy in his sight, without blemish and free from accusation."* Colossians 1: 21-22.

The same Holy Spirit of God that raised Jesus from death to life will do the same for you. That is what God promises us in His new will, *"For my Father's will is that everyone who looks to the Son and believes in him shall have eternal life, and I will raise him up at the last day."* John 6:40.

Do you want real peace in your life? Do you want to live for a real purpose? Do you want freedom from a life that has you in bondage to sin?

It could be alcohol, drug addiction, pornography, or an angry unforgiving nature. Whatever Satan has you slave to, Jesus will set you free from that sin and the burden that has enslaved you. You cannot buy this with money. The cost to you is you turning away from your old sinful life and beginning a brand new life with Christ's spirit inside you.

Maybe you thought you were saved and now you're not sure or maybe you ran away from God like I did, in my teens. Then eight years ago, I was rescued by pilot Jesus who threw me a rope ladder that I hooked in to and He extracted me from a heavy canopy jungle of sin. Or maybe you have never met Him.

Today, you have been introduced to Jesus. He loves you and no matter what you've done, He died for you and will forgive you from all your guilt and sins. If you want to establish a relationship with Jesus all you need to do is ask, from your heart, for Jesus to forgive you from all your sins. He is faithful and just. He is obligated to forgive you no matter what you've done in the past.

The very moment you accept Jesus as your Savior, the bondage of being a slave to Satan and sin is removed from you, **you're Free!** Jesus said, *"...you shall know the truth and the truth shall set you free."* John 8:32.

Who's Your Daddy?

We are under a spiritual contract right now. Either we are under the Almighty God, Yahweh's contract, which states Jesus is the way to the Father, *"I am the way and the truth and the life. No one comes to the Father except through me."* John 14:6. Or we are under the Devil's spiritual contract as Jesus declared to us in John, *"You belong to **your father**, the **devil**, and* *you want to carry out **your father's** desire. He was a murderer from the beginning, not holding to the truth, for there is no truth in him. When he lies, he speaks his native language, for he is a liar and the **father** of lies."* John 8:44.

Please understand that Jesus' defeat of Satan, his forces, and his works only effects those that love, believe, and obey God and have accepted Jesus as their Savior, those who have begun a new life. If you don't believe in God's Son Jesus, then Satan will always remain your daddy.

God wants us to build upon the victory Jesus gave us and to advance the kingdom of heaven by capturing souls for the Kingdom. To accomplish this goal, Jesus gave us spiritual weapons revealed to us through the Word of God. In addition, Jesus also gave us other spiritual gifts that empower us to accomplish what God has planned for us in spiritual warfare.

If you think you can sit on the fence and remain neutral, indeed you can, but that territory belongs to Satan. Uncommitted soldiers are referred to as luke-warm soldiers. God will have nothing to do with us if we are lukewarm. He'll spit us out of His mouth. Jesus tells us in Revelations, *"I know your deeds, that you are neither cold nor hot. I wish you were either one or the other! So, because you are lukewarm—neither hot nor cold—I am about to spit you out of my mouth."*(Revelations 3: 15-16).

We need to surrender and when I say surrender, I use the term in the same way an enemy soldier would. We need to give up our life and desires for ourselves and depend unequivocally on God for His plan and His will in our life. Our lives should be all about God and the Kingdom of God and doing His Will not ours.

One picture firmly imprinted in my memory is that of enemy soldiers captured as prisoners of war, or those who surrendered holding the pamphlet that we dropped from aircrafts guaranteeing any enemy soldier who surrendered to us a new life of freedom. The words on the flyer were guaranteed by the United States Armed Services. In both instances, the picture is the same. The enemy was captured as prisoners or they gave up, they clearly indicated their surrender with their hands and arms shooting straight up high into the air in total surrender. In their eyes was extreme fear, they shook all over and some wet themselves. Others were too weak in the knees and couldn't stand up; they fell to the ground on their knees in a state of fear. Their faith was in us keeping to our word. They knew because their life was spared that they now had to give their remaining life to those that spared them and took them as prisoners.

They really gave up; they surrendered and meant it from their heart. Many of them would start telling you whatever information you asked for. Some were selected to go through a pacification program and joined with U.S. Recon teams serving as scouts and pathfinders. They became some of the best soldiers we had.

God expects the very same from you and I. To surrender our lives means we give up our remaining life and start a new life living with and for God. We bring promises of the words containing God's promises; we add our belief and faith in Jesus from our hearts and we surrender.

We are just like the Prisoners of War in Vietnam. We all have scars and scar tissue of our life's struggles. We all have wounds - some are old and have never healed. We need to bring them with our arms straight up in the air toward God, come to the throne of God and place them at the feet of Jesus and say, "I surrender all. I give you myself; save my soul, heal my wounds, clean me up so I can see Jesus and have a relationship with Him and Father God."

Salvation is a day to day life style between you and God. God has a predestined plan for you.

If you don't have a relationship with God, if you don't protect that relationship, how will you determine who and what God wants for you? Everything you expect God to do for you is conditional on your relationship with Him.

A Relationship - Not an Affair

One thing you can bet on, I built a relationship with my Army Ranger trainer Tad. I listened to him. I acted like him; I ate what he ate. I walked like he walked, I talked like he talked, I painted my face camouflaged like he painted his, I thought like he thought, I dressed like he dressed and I visualized the what if's he taught us to visualize, so we could react and survive when under extreme fire power and out-numbered by the enemy. Once the gun fire begins and you're out numbered 7 to 1, you suddenly realize you need help. You wonder how fast they'll come. You wonder if they will come at all. It's during times like these that you wonder who's got your back. Who do you have backing you up?

In Vietnam, Tad was my mentor. I listened, I believed, I acted in obedience to his teachings. Tad was an expert in guerrilla warfare. Looking back, I believe God put me where I had the best training available, it was up to me to listen. It was up to me to learn. It was my decision to believe or not and it was my choice to obey.

If I had just been friendly with Tad, instead of establishing a relationship, I would have listened when I wanted to. I would have selected what I liked and rejected what I didn't like. If I had done what I felt like doing, the results would be the questions that I hear people everywhere asking, including inside churches, "Why does God allow these things to happen?" If you try to have an affair with God, instead of having a relationship with Him, you will always be asking this question. "Why does God allow this to happen?" But, if you surrender your all, your life you have left to live is not for this world because we're just passing through. Our life belongs to God.

If you build your relationship with the heavenly Father, the Holy Spirit will teach you to walk as Jesus walked, to eat what He ate, to visualize what He taught, to obey His teachings. Your heart will be clean and your motives for your actions will be for Him, not you; you'll be in the vine producing fruit. Then, when you get in trouble and call out in Jesus Name, you'll realize and see who's got your back.

This is exactly what you and I need to do with Jesus. It's not too late. God loves you and wants you now! There is nothing that you have done that God hasn't already forgiven you for.

Why are you waiting? You're not too old. What have you got to lose? Your soul?

God the Father loves you. He wants you to fall in love with Him. Jesus promises He'll never leave you nor run when your back is turned. He needs you to just trust in Him, to spend time with Him in prayer, to surrender and volunteer your life as a soldier serving in the Army of God for "the Kingdom of heaven."

I believe the greatest word in the English language is the word Redeem. Redeem means, "to buy back"; another meaning is, "to save from captivity by paying a ransom." Back in Moses' time, one way to buy back a slave was to offer an equivalent or superior slave in exchange.

That is the way God chose to buy you and me back. He offered His Son Jesus in exchange for you and me for our lives. You must understand that for you and me to be free from the deadly consequences of our sins, a tremendous price must be paid. A price we are unable and cannot pay. The only thing superior to us is God the Father, His Son Jesus, and the Holy Spirit of God.

So, God sent His only Son Jesus, as our substitute to pay the Redeeming Price for you and me for our sins, the death penalty sentence. Jesus gave His life so that you and I may live a life more abundantly, meaning freedom from the bondage and slavery of the prince of this world, Satan.

Your Secret Weapon

Each day that goes by may be our last. Like in Vietnam, we're in a battle, only today it is with our spiritual enemy Satan. Your secret weapon is Jesus. The chopper is here to extract you up out of the sinful nature you're in. The enemy is telling you no, maybe next time; there is always another chance. He is a liar and a thief.

Jesus just dropped the rope ladder down through the thick layer of sinful canopy that you thought couldn't be penetrated. You had lost hope and were about to give up, but just hadn't told anyone. It's hanging there waiting for you to decide whether to accept a life with Christ and hook up with Him or continue in your fake and perceived happy life you're living, without real purpose.

Jesus is knocking on your hearts' door saying, "Hook up with me. I'll save your soul and change your life. I'll give you a real purpose to live for. I'll give you real peace and a reason to live for." It's really simple. You can ask Jesus to meet you and forgive you right now. Just say this prayer from your heart and mean it.

"Heavenly Father, in your Son's name Jesus, I believe and accept your plan of salvation for me. From the bottom of my heart, I say I'm sorry for living my life in sin.

I confess all the sins that I can remember and those that I cannot remember to You. Please remove them from me like You said You would. Your word says that the moment I confess my sins, they're gone. You remove them as far as the East is from the West.

I believe that Jesus is the Son of God and that His blood has just removed every sin I ever committed; because He died for me. I want Jesus' promise to free me, so I can start all over with Him.

Father God, I believe from my heart that Jesus died for me. I believe Jesus was raised from the dead by Your Holy Spirit's power and is alive at Your right hand side sitting on the throne. Jesus, save me, a sinner lost.

I love you Father God. I need you and I want you. Please send Your Holy Spirit into me to come and live within me to sanctify and cleanse me. I desire this from my heart and mean every word.

I give to you all I have to give, which is me, the remaining life that You allow me to live. I want to live it, seeking You so I can know You more. I want to please you!

I'm yours; keep me in the Vine, which is Jesus. Protect me. I want a relationship with you, Father.

Thank you Jesus for saving me! *You're my* ***Secret Weapon."***

If you confess with your mouth, "Jesus is Lord," and believe in your heart that God raised him from the dead, you will be saved. For it is with your heart that you believe and are justified, and it is with your mouth that you confess and are saved. As the Scripture says, "Anyone who trusts in him will never be put to shame." "For there is no difference between Jew and Gentile— the same Lord is Lord of all and richly blesses all who call on him, for, "Everyone who calls on the name of the Lord will be saved." Romans 10: 9-13.

You have a free will. The choice is yours.

God loves you, and you'll realize just how much when you see Him in heaven, standing before Him as He judges you individually, as Jesus gives you your rewards for your behavior you accomplished while on planet Earth.

Will you be able to stand?

Will you fall to the ground in fear?

Will you weep with love?

Will you be escorted out of the Kingdom?

If this book has blessed you, please tell someone so they can share in God's blessed salvation. Bless someone with a gift by giving them a copy of this book. And please email me and tell me what He has done for you. If you need prayer email me at: danny@ziongarden.org.

Brother,
Danny Clifford

Author's Testimony

In my youth, I was brought up in a Church that taught about Jesus Christ and the kingdom of heaven, but lacked teaching on the Holy Spirit. Very little understanding of whom the Holy Spirit was and certainly no teaching that the Holy Spirit was active today with miracles, Signs, and wonders. To believe that God would heal someone was good and to pray for them to be healed, if it was God's will, is what we were taught. Most of the time, it wasn't God's will; I don't remember anyone ever being healed.

In my sophomore year in High School, I traded my relationship with God and my plans to serve God for popularity, pride, and worldly friends. My success in high school baseball and football and later on American Legion and town team baseball, my pride and ego replaced anything I had left for God. By my senior year, smoking and drinking were among some of my habits and I was far from my relationship with God, unless I got in trouble.

The change from seeking to do God's will, when I was 6-8 grader, to desiring the pleasures of the sinful nature and enjoying the worldly environment was a subtle, smooth transition. Once I decided to do it, it became easier and easier to justify to myself.

After I graduated from High School, I volunteered for the U. S. Army. I spent 18 months in Vietnam as an Airborne Ranger running reconnaissance missions. I came out of the service and was married. I chased the dreams and goals of the world. I allowed Corporations, companies, and Satan's worldly system to dictate what my purpose for life was, thus defining success for me, and finally setting my goals.

The moral, ethical, and spiritual teachings that I received in my early years in church were altered, twisted, and or replaced by what seemed to be a much more lucrative sounding promise for life, which affected my belief and behavior.

The Spirit of God was still speaking to my soul, but my soul just wouldn't listen; it sided with my natural self. I was under the influence and control of the Prince of this world. He had me right where he wanted me.

I was accepted by the world, I was somebody or so I thought. I left and wanted no part of God unless I got into trouble, then I needed Him for a short time and would leave Him again. I did encourage my children, once in a while, to go to church when they were young, but I really didn't put any priority in their upbringing in God. Thank God, my Mother took them to church whenever she could. I thought, like the rest of the world, God would look after us; He'd take care of me; I was one of His. He's a God of Love, maybe there would be time later for God, or that's what I thought.

You see, what I really wanted was to have an affair with Jesus and God. But God wanted to have a relationship with me. To sum it up, I was an Ideal sinner, one of Satan's best. Now, the Holy Spirit was actively pursuing me although I didn't know it.

In the fall of 2002, I had just gone through a divorce after a marriage of 31 years. I was living in a rented apartment; I had an automobile not worth what I owed on it and about $12,000 in credit card debt. I did have a job and was able pay my bills. I was humbled. I was broke in spirit, in finances, and in purpose for living. I was drinking, smoking; I was headed out into the world looking for more sin. I was chasing love from women, something I thought had escaped me in life. Physical love from a woman, that's what I wanted before I died and I intended to get some. Sin was not a concern.

I remember, coming home from work, I would pour myself a drink of scotch and water to relax and smoke some cigarettes before fixing my dinner. I don't know why, but I began to read the Bible and watch some Christian programs on T.V. I came under heavy conviction, by the Holy Spirit, of my sins and sinful life against God. While I was drinking and smoking, the Holy Spirit began convicting me of my past 40 years of running away from God.

He told me that God wanted me to come back to Him. That God loved me and no matter how many prostitutes, no matter how many beers, no matter how many drugs, no matter the divorce, no matter what, God loved me just the way I was and wanted me, just as I was, to surrender my life to Him. The Holy Spirit told me, "I'll pick you up out of the gutter of sin. I'll extract you out from the thick jungle canopy of slavery and sin.

I'll wash you with clean purified water. I'll cleanse you in the Blood of Jesus and teach you what to do.

My soul could hear God. In my quiet apartment, I began to pray. "God, I know You're real and I know I'm a sinner and have lived a life of sin against You. I was ashamed of You and Your teachings and I turned my back on You when I chose my school friends and the life style of the world versus what You offered and wanted me to do. In spite of what I did to You, all during my life, whenever I got in real trouble, You always took care of me, sometimes before I called on You.

My mind quickly flashed back 25 years to when my daughter was in the hospital turning blue dying from lack of oxygen while two doctors were trying to decide whether to wait for the new miracle drug they had given her to take effect or to perform a tracheotomy on her so she could breath. God saved her life. My mind flashed back to the present and how ashamed I felt because God was always willing to accept me just the way I was.

In February of 2003, I committed to God to give myself totally to Him. I promised God I would surrender my All to Him. I asked God to show me the same Jesus that walked on the earth 2000 years ago performing miracles. I asked Him to allow me to see souls saved and lives changed; healing by an alive - living Holy Spirit because I really believe you are the same today as you were 2000 years ago.

I wasn't talking about me hearing about or seeing on T.V. I asked Him to be a carrier of the Holy Spirit and of having an anointing to serve Him in a capacity where I would witness and participate in seeing the Holy Spirit of God move and work signs, wonders, and miracles.

The first miracle God did was save my Soul from Hell, after all the sin I had committed against him, God forgave me. Not only did God forgive me, He allowed me to see the young man in Trinidad, who couldn't walk, come up out of the wheel chair and walk. God did what I asked for and so much more.

God gave me a purpose, a mission. I have the privilege to introduce to you **Jesus Christ,** the undisputed **Savior** of the World -**The Messiah.**

He loves you and wants to meet you. He wants you to establish a relationship with Him.

Breinigsville, PA USA
20 January 2011
253713BV00003B/1/P